War in the Persian Gulf
Reference Library
Cumulative Index

War in the Persian Gulf
Reference Library
Cumulative Index

From Operation Desert Storm
to Operation Iraqi Freedom

Cumulates Indexes For:

War in the Persian Gulf Almanac
War in the Persian Gulf Biographies
War in the Persian Gulf Primary Sources

Julie Carnagie,
Project Editor

U·X·L
An imprint of Thomson Gale,
a part of The Thomson Corporation

THOMSON
GALE

Detroit • New York • San Francisco • San Diego • New Haven, Conn. • Waterville, Maine • London • Munich

War in the Persian Gulf Reference Library Cumulative Index:
From Operation Desert Storm to Operation Iraqi Freedom

Project Editor
Julie L. Carnagie

Permissions
Shalice Shah-Caldwell,
Margaret Chamberlain

Imaging and Multimedia
Lezlie Light, Mike Logusz, Christine
O'Bryan, Kelly A. Quin

Product Design
Pamela Galbreath

Composition
Evi Seoud

Manufacturing
Rita Wimberley

Printed in the United States of America
10 9 8 7 6 5 4 3 2 1
ISBN 0-7876-9111-9
This title is also available as an e-book. ISBN 0-7876-9347-2
Contact your Gale sales representative for ordering information.

Cumulative Index

A = War in the Persian Gulf Almanac
B = War in the Persian Gulf Biographies
PS = War in the Persian Gulf Primary Sources

Bold type indicates set titles, main biographical entries, and their page numbers. Illustrations are marked by (ill.).

Geneva Conventions
   A 16, 59–60
   B 264
Glaspie, April
   A 21
   B 135–40, 135 (ill.), 254
   PS 1–13, 12 (ill.)
Gorbachev, Mikhail
   A 62–64
   B 9, 238
Gore, Al
   B 76–77
Graham, Billy
   A 113
   B 75
Great Britain
   B support for United
     States during 1991 Per-
     sian Gulf War 50–52
   B support for United
     States during 2003 Iraq
     War 246–47
Gulf Cooperation Council
   A 40
Gulf War syndrome
   A 81
   B 121–24, 225, 266

H

Hakim, Muhammad Bakar
   al-
   A 161, 167
Halliday, Denis
   A 97
Hashimi, Aquila al-
   A 170
Heath, Ted
   B 245
Holliman, John
   B 21, 25
   PS 45–46, 49–52
Howe, Sir G.
   A 27 (ill.)
Human shields
   A 32–34, 35 (ill.), 43
Hussein ibn Talal
   A 21, 27, 29, 29 (ill.), 42
   B 9, 141–48, 141 (ill.),
     146 (ill.), 238
   PS 15–24, 17 (ill.)
Hussein, Qusay

   A 113, 119, 121 (ill.),
     165–66, 167 (ill.)
   B 151
Hussein, Saddam
   A 1, 11 (ill.), 15 (ill.), 29
     (ill.), 35 (ill.), 66, 121
     (ill.), 130, 131 (ill.)
   A capture of 171–72, 171
     (ill.)
   A crushes 1991 uprisings
     85–88
   A decision to invade
     Kuwait 18–22, 30–31
   A and Iran-Iraq War 14,
     16
   A palaces of 139
   A reaction to UN weapons
     inspections and eco-
     nomic sanctions
     98–101, 113–16
   A removed from power
     142–43
   A rise to power 7, 9–12
   B 16 (ill.), 24, 27–28,
     32–34, 38, 41, 49, 52,
     56, 67, 69, 73, 78, 80,
     96, 98, 146 (ill.),
     149–59, 149 (ill.), 158
     (ill.), 188, 191, 195,
     212, 222, 236, 266
   B capture of 61, 158–59
   B decision to invade
     Kuwait 135–38, 153–54,
     205–06
   B Iraqi opposition to 85
   B meeting with U.S. Am-
     bassador April Glaspie
     137–39, 254
   B meeting with U.S. Am-
     bassador Joseph Wilson
     254–55
   B as a military leader 224
   B popularity among Pales-
     tinians 15, 145–46
   PS **1–13**, 3 (ill.), 18, 45,
     104, 107
   PS decision to invade
     Kuwait 1–13
   PS as a military leader 72
   PS removed from power
     96, 99–100
   PS and weapons of mass
     destruction 86, 88

Hussein, Uday
   A 99–100, 113, 119, 121
     (ill.), 165–66, 167 (ill.)
   B 151, 213

I

IAEA. *See* International
   Atomic Energy Agency
*I Am a Soldier, Too: The Jessi-
   ca Lynch Story*
   B 167
IGC. *See* Iraq Governing
   Council (IGC)
INC. *See* Iraqi National Con-
   gress
International Atomic Energy
   Agency (IAEA)
   A 90
Intifada
   B 14, 230
Iran
   A 14–18, 32
   B 2, 205
Iran-Iraq War
   A 14–18, 17 (ill.)
   B 34, 136, 145, 152, 205
   PS 2
Iraq
   A borders of 4–5
   A civilian casualties in 61,
     63, 76, 97–98, 133
   A damage from 1991 Per-
     sian Gulf War 83–84, 86
     (ill.)
   A early history of 3
   A economic sanctions
     against 30, 40–41
   A guerilla tactics used in
     2003 Iraq War 128,
     132–33
   A military performance in
     1991 Persian Gulf War
     59, 70–71, 75–76
   A 1990 invasion of
     Kuwait 23–25, 25 (ill),
     34–36
   A 1991 uprisings in 85–87
   A no-fly zones in 90–92,
     93 (ill.)

A search for weapons of mass destruction in 159, 162, 164

A postwar reconstruction of 151–75

A postwar security problems in 155, 166–67, 169 (ill.)

A resistance to U.S. military buildup 50 (ill.)

A resistance to U.S. occupation 157 (ill.), 158–59

A transfer of political power in 169–70

A treatment of coalition prisoners of war 59–60, 129 (ill.), 130

A unconditional surrender of 74 (ill.)

A UN economic sanctions against 93–99, 95 (ill.)

A UN weapons inspections in 89–92, 100–02, 100 (ill.), 105 (ill.), 108–09

A use of chemical weapons 16–17

A use of foreign citizens as "human shields" 32–34, 35 (ill.), 43

B 1991 uprisings in 155–56

B postwar reconstruction of 57–61, 81, 106, 200, 260

B postwar security problems in 52, 57–61, 81, 189, 200, 258

B resistance to U.S. occupation 60, 81, 158, 189, 200, 258

B treatment of coalition prisoners of war 238–39, 262–64, 266

B treatment of Kuwaiti citizens during occupation of Kuwait 207, 209

B United Nations economic sanctions against 156, 185, 213

B United Nations weapons inspections in 37, 50, 79, 156–57, 177, 213

B use of chemical weapons against Kurdish population 153

B use of foreign citizens as "human shields" 255

B weapons of mass destruction in 37, 50–52, 98, 156–57, 177, 188–89, 195, 253, 258–59

PS damage from 1991 Persian Gulf War 61 (ill.), 68 (ill.)

PS damage from 2003 Iraq War 100 (ill.), 106–07

PS economic sanctions against 4–5

PS military performance during 1991 Persian Gulf War 72

PS 1990 invasion of Kuwait 1–6, 11–12

PS postwar reconstruction of 105–06, 114 (ill.)

PS postwar security problems in 93, 101, 108 (ill.)

PS use of chemical weapons 3

PS U.S. military occupation of 113, 117 (ill.)

Iraq Governing Council (IGC)
  A 163–65, 170
  B 60, 87, 90

Iraqi army
  PS mass surrenders during 1991 Persian Gulf War 77–81

Iraqi Army Lieutenant's Diary
  PS 55–64

Iraqi National Accord
  A 161

Iraqi National Congress (INC)
  A 161
  B 83, 85

Iraqi opposition groups
  A 160–61

Iraqi resistance
  A 158–59

Iraq War, opposition to
  A 116–17, 117 (ill.)

Islam
  A 2
  B 126

Israel
  A 28, 31, 42
  A and Iraq's missile attacks against during 1991 Persian Gulf War 56–58
  B 12, 14, 142, 147, 155, 227, 229
  B decision not to enter the 1991 Persian Gulf War 231
  PS 16–17, 34

Israeli-Palestinian conflict
  B 12–14, 18–19, 142–43, 229–30

It Doesn't Take a Hero
  B 225

"It's Not Too Late to Prevent a War"
  PS 15–24

J

Jackson, Jesse
  A 34

Jafari, Ibrahim al-
  A 174

Japanese internment camps
  PS 28–29

John Paul II, Pope
  A 96–97
  B 37

Jordan
  B history of 142–44
  B Palestinian population of 144
  B support of Iraq during 1991 Persian Gulf War 145–46
  PS 16, 21–22
  PS and refugee crisis during 1991 Persian Gulf War 22 (ill.), 23

K

Kent, Arthur
  B 6–7

Khafji, battle of
A 66-68, 69 (ill.)
Khomeini, Ayatollah Ruhollah
A 14, 17
B 2, 34, 152
King Hussein of Jordan. *See*
Hussein ibn Talal
Kurdish refugee crisis
B 5
Kurdistan Democratic Party
(KDP)
A 160
Kurds
A 3, 17, 19 (ill.), 85–87, 87
(ill.), 99, 144, 160, 165
B 5, 153, 156
Kuwait
A 16
A damage from 1991 Persian Gulf War 79–83, 83
(ill.)
A early history of 3–4, 6–7
A Iraq's 1990 invasion of
21–25, 25 (ill.)
A Iraq's occupation of 30,
34–36, 36 (ill.)
A liberation of 71–72, 73
(ill.)
A oil industry in 20
A oil well fires in 58, 80,
84 (ill.)
B 35, 137, 153
B damage from 1991 Persian Gulf War 207–09
B history of 203–04
B Palestinian population
of 15
B resistance to Iraqi occupation 208–10
B suffering under Iraqi occupation 207
PS 8
PS Iraq's 1990 invasion of
18
PS Iraq's occupation of
37, 57 (ill.)
PS liberation of 70 (ill.)
PS oil well fires in 77–78
Kuwaiti resistance
A 35–36, 83

L

Labour Party (U.K.)
B 47–48
Lehi (Lohamei Eretz Yisrael,
"Fighters for the Freedom of Israel")
B 228
*Live from the Battlefield:
From Vietnam to Baghdad—35 Years in the
World's War Zones*
B 28
PS 45–54
Lohamei Eretz Yisrael. *See*
Lehi
Lou Gehrig's disease. *See*
Amyotrophic lateral
sclerosis (ALS)
Lowey, Nita
A 98
Lynch, Jessica
A 136
B 161–68, 161, (ill.), 166
(ill.)

M

Majid, Ali Hassan al-
A 140–41
Major, John
B 247–49
Mandela, Nelson
A 116
McChrystal, Stanley
A 145
Media censorship. *See* U.S.
military, censorship of
media coverage during
1991 Persian Gulf War
Media coverage
B of the 1991 Persian Gulf
War 5–7, 21, 25–28, 237
B of the 2003 Iraq War
215
Mesopotamia
A 3
PS 4–5
Metzenbaum, Howard
A 19–20
Middle East
A map of 6 (ill.)

Middle East peace process
B 17–19, 147, 232–33
Milosevic, Slobodan
B 6, 48, 103–04
Mitterand, Francois
B 103
Moth, Margaret
B 8
Mubarak, Hosni
A 21
Muhammad (prophet)
A 2, 3 (ill.)
Muslim Americans
PS 25–26, 29 (ill.), 33
(ill.), 34
Muslims
A 2
My American Journey
B 176
Myers, Richard
A 132

N

Nahyan, Zaid al-
A 97
*Naked in Baghdad: The
Iraq War as Seen by
NPR's Correspondent*
PS 95–102
Nasiriyah, Iraq
A 128
B 164–65
National Public Radio (NPR)
PS 95
National Security Council
(NSC)
B 186, 259
National Security Strategy
B 188
Nawa, Fariba
PS 25–34
Netanyahu, Benjamin
B 17
News coverage. *See* Media
coverage
Nicols, John
B 263
Nixon, Richard
B 40, 66
Nobel Peace Prize
B 17

No-fly zones
  A 90–92
Noor, Queen of Jordan
  PS 23
Noriega, Manuel
  B 95–96, 173
NPR. *See* National Public
  Radio
NSC. *See* National Security
  Council

O

Oil
  A as a factor in the 1991
    Persian Gulf War 46
  PS as a factor in the 1991
    Persian Gulf War 37
Oil-for-food program
  A 96
OPEC. *See* Organization of
  Oil Exporting Countries
Operation Desert Fox
  A 101–02
Operation Desert Shield
  A 28, 37–40, 49, 53
  B 97, 111, 119, 173–74,
    198, 255
Operation Desert Storm
  A 53–76, 72 (ill.)
  A air war 53–63, 55 (ill.),
    57 (ill.), 62 (ill.)
  A ground war 65–76, 67
    (ill.), 71 (ill.)
  A live television coverage
    of 55–56
  B 69, 97, 112, 119, 174,
    198, 223, 247–48, 255
  PS 36–37, 40–42, 41 (ill.)
  PS air war 49–52, 55–64,
    66
  PS coalition military strat-
    egy in 65–71
  PS ground war 63, 66–71,
    75, 76 (ill.), 80 (ill.)
  PS live television coverage
    of 42, 45, 47, 49–53, 51
    (ill.)
Operation Enduring Free-
  dom
  A 106
  B 78, 194–95, 198–99

Operation Iraqi Freedom
  A 119–46, 133 (ill.), 147
    (ill.)
  A capture of Baghdad 136,
    137 (ill.), 141–44, 143
    (ill.)
  A criticism of military
    strategy 131–33
  A news coverage of
    124–25
  A "shock and awe" bomb-
    ing campaign 126–27
  A U.S. casualties in 168
  A "wave of steel" ground
    campaign 127–28, 127
    (ill.)
  B 80, 189, 191, 197
  PS capture of Baghdad 96,
    99–100, 105
  PS news coverage of 95,
    97, 101–03, 110
  PS U.S. military perfor-
    mance during 115
Operation Just Cause
  B 96
Operation Thunder Run
  A 138–39
Organization of Oil Export-
  ing Countries (OPEC)
  A 20, 22
  B 35, 137, 204
  PS 2–3
Oslo Accord
  B 17
Ottoman Empire
  A 3–4
  PS 56

P

Pahlavi, Mohammed Reza,
  Shah of Iran
  B 2
Palacio, Ana
  A 110
Palestine
  B 228
Palestine Liberation Organi-
  zation (PLO)
  A 28
  B 11, 13–15, 18, 143,
    145–46, 229

B support of Iraq during
  1991 Persian Gulf War
  11, 15–17
B terrorist activities of 13
PS 16, 18
Palestinian Authority
  B 17–18
Palestinians
  A 28, 31, 82
  B 12, 15, 142, 144, 147,
    229
  PS 16–17, 34
Panama
  B 95–96, 173
Path to Power, The
  B 250
Patriotic Union of Kurdistan
  (PUK)
  A 160
Patriot missiles
  A 57–58
Pax, Salam
  PS 111–20
Peres, Shimon
  B 17, 230
Peters, John
  B 263
Piestewa, Lori
  B 163–64
Plame, Valerie
  B 259
PLO. *See* Palestine Liberation
  Organization
Pompidou, Georges
  B 102
Powell, Alma
  B 265 (ill.)
Powell, Colin
  A 33 (ill.), 41 (ill.),
    108–09, 111 (ill.)
  B 68 (ill.), 77, **169–79**,
    169 (ill.), 175 (ill.), 183,
    186, 224 (ill.), 265 (ill.)
POWs. *See* Prisoners of war
  (POWs)
Presidential Medal of Free-
  dom
  B 44, 176, 193, 225, 250
Primakov, Yevgeny
  A 101
Prisoners of war (POWs)
  B 109, 113, 164–65, 235,
    238–39, 261–64